Boops' Character Missions

Mission I: Roatan

Bron Chapman, John Chapman & Leslie Chapman

To order additional copies of this book, contact:
Xlibris
844-714-8691
www.Xlibris.com
Orders@Xlibris.com

ISBN: Softcover   978-1-6641-5081-2
       EBook   978-1-6641-5080-5

Print information available on the last page

Rev. date: 01/07/2021

Acknowledgements

To Voncile Chapman, thank you for your support of this book, and for creating the educational activities. To Anjanette Sullivan, thank you for the curriculum you designed to supplement the content covered in this book.

To my mother, Eunice Austin and father, Neville Austin (deceased). Thank you for the family trips which created the desire in a little girl to want to travel the world.

Hi, my name is Boops. I live with my papa, Boonks, and my mama, Baps, in a village called Hodgepodge. In Hodgepodge, kids like me learn ten character traits from the elders of our village.

The elders send each child on a mission all over the world to find these wonderful character traits. The missions are exciting because I learn about cultures, meet different people, and learn about their traditions, all by exploring with my parents!

My very first mission is to an island in the
Caribbean called Roatan. I am so excited! I do
not know much about Roatan, and I wonder
if it's anything like Hodgepodge. Mama gets
our travel plans while Papa prepares the heli-
camper for takeoff. I pack my backpack, and I
am ready to go.

Papa starts the heli-camper and we all shout, "1-Mississippi, 2-Mississippi, 3-Mississippi, GO!"

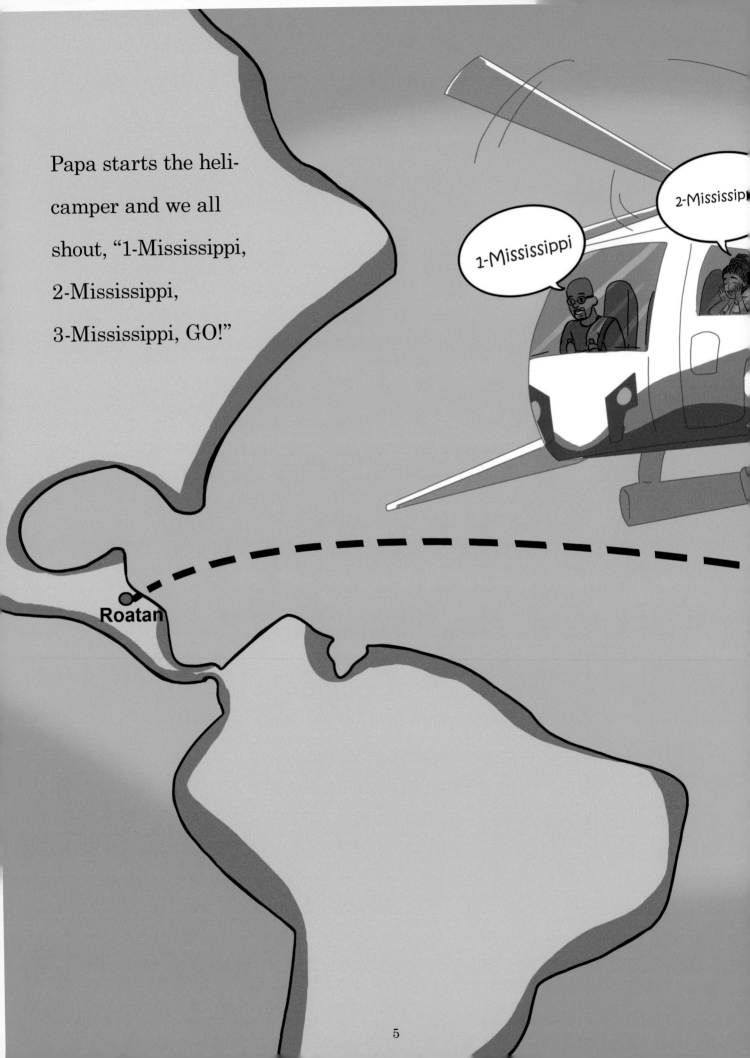

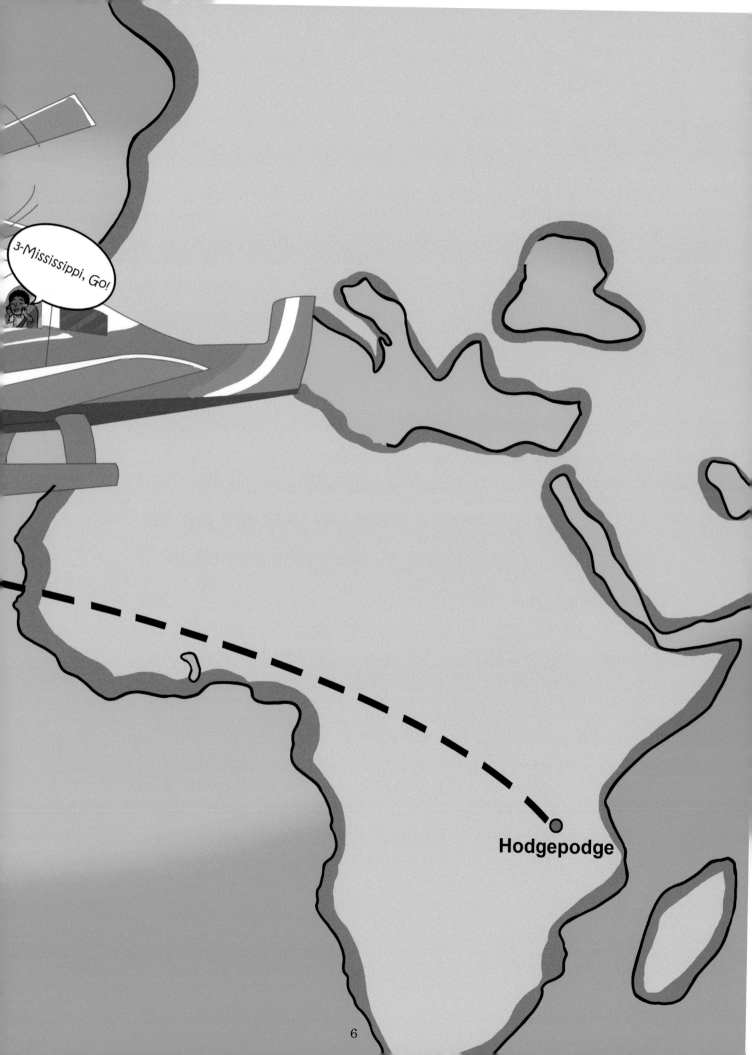

"Hello! Hola! Welcome to Roatan Boops," says Yasmen. "Your first mission is to discover why you have been sent to Roatan. Good luck Boops!"

I am so nervous. I really want to know why the elders have sent me to Roatan and solve this mission.

"Do not worry son, Papa says. "Your Mama and I are here to help you."

"That's right!" says Yasmen, "Let's start!"

"First, we will hike down from here and head into a city called Coxen Hole," Yasmen says.

"Sounds good to me," I say. We hike down a little trail that leads to Coxen Hole. Roatan is beautiful.

"Those are yellow-naped parrots chirping up in the tall, green palm trees!" says Yasmen.

Then, I hear the sound of music coming from up ahead!

COXEN HOLE

We see three boys playing drums with their hands. I do not know what they are singing, but it sounds funny.

"These are the Garifuna people and they are welcoming you to their village in their native language; Spanish," says Yasmen.

"Here, hand this tip to the boys," says Papa.

I throw the money at their feet.

Yasmen looks displeased at what I've done.

"In our culture, throwing something at someone is a lack of respect," says Yasmen. I don't really pay too much attention to what she says. I just laugh and begin to dance to the music. I can see Mama is not happy with my behavior.

"Boops what are you doing! Yasmen is speaking to you," says Mama. Papa and Yasmen both look disappointed. I worry that solving this mission may be harder than I thought.

"Let's go see the dolphins," says Yasmen.

We board the bus and head to Dolphin Encounter at Sandy Bay. Papa takes me to go change.

"Boops, what you did was not funny at all," Papa begins. "By throwing the tip at those boys, you showed a lack of respect for their culture. Then you ignored Yasmen when she explained this to you by laughing and dancing."

"I didn't mean to Papa, I was just trying to have fun," I say.

"I know you didn't do it on purpose," Papa replies. "You see, culture is very important."

I keep hearing that word culture. I am not sure what it really means, so I ask Papa to explain it to me.

"It is made of many different things," he begins. "Some things that make up a culture are food, clothes, music and language. Each culture is different."

"I see what you mean Papa," I say. "Back home in Hodgepodge you eat pizza, but here in Roatan you eat a lot of that fish with the weird name."

"Yes, sort of Boops, it is called Chilean sea bass" Papa says, "but more importantly, culture also includes how we treat people. Here in Roatan, drums are played to greet people. It's their way of welcoming visitors to their country. We give them a tip to show our appreciation."

"I understand now Papa," I say. "I am very sorry."

"I'm glad you're beginning to learn about respecting culture," Papa says with a smile. "It is very important for this mission! Now, let's go meet up with your Mama and Yasmen to see the dolphins."

I get my swim fins and snorkel gear, and we
walk into the refreshing crystal-clear water.
Yasmen is in front of us with a dolphin.

"This is Callie," says Yasmen. "Try to whistle for her to come to you Boops!"

I whistle and Callie swims right up to me so I can pet her. She feels so slippery and wet. Callie disappears under the water and emerges with a box that was buried under the sand below.

"What is that?" I ask.

"It is for you," says Yasmen.

I open the box and inside is a large seashell.
I hold it to my ear, and I am certain I hear a
voice coming from the shell.

"Oh no!" I yell. I almost drop the shell.
"Yasmen! Yasmen! I hear a voice!"

Yasmen does not seem rattled. She just smiles
at me.

"Well, what do you hear?" Yasmen asks.

"I think I hear the word respect; but, I'm not
sure I know what that word means?" I say.
I wonder, could this be a clue as to why the
elders sent me to Roatan?

Mama walks toward me. "Boops, would you like to know what respect means?" she asks. I nod my head.

"Respect means that you act in a way that shows you care about others feelings and well-being," she explains. "Like when Papa told you to respect the culture of the Garifuna people."

I think I am beginning to understand. "I was not showing respect when I laughed and danced when we saw the three boys singing," I say.

"Yes!" says Yasmen excitedly. "This was your mission Boops— to learn what respect means. In my culture, we say el respeto! Keep this seashell because it represents one of the ten character traits that you will find on your missions. Good luck and safe travels!"

I feel very proud that I solved my first mission. I also learned a new word: *respeto*. As I continue on my missions around the world, I am determined to show respect to all people, and their culture.

I want you to join me. Are you ready to help me with these missions? Well, what are we waiting for...

1-Mississippi

2-Mississippi,

3-Mississippi,

GO!

4 FACTS ABOUT ROATAN

ROATAN IS AN ISLAND

Even though Roatan is part of Honduras, it isn't connected to it. Instead Roatan is are surrounded by water in the Caribbean Sea.

THE HONDURAS FLAG

This the official flag for the country of Honduras. The two blue stripes represent the Pacific Ocean and the Caribbean Sea that neighbor the country on both sides!

PEOPLE LOVE TO GO DIVING

The geographic location of Roatan allows the people access the ocean for activities such as diving, snorkeling and other water adventures.

THE GARIFUNA DRUMS

Garifuna drums are an important part of the Garifuna Peoples' music culture. There are two drums, one is called the primero and the other the segunda.

Crossword Activity Fun

ACROSS

3 A leader or senior figure in a group of people
7 Boops' village
8 An island in Honduras
9 Boops' mother

DOWN

1 The food, music, clothes, and language a group of people share
2 An important assignment
4 The way you act that shows you care about others' feelings and well-being
5 Boops' father
6 The main character on this mission

WWW.PUZZLE-MAKER.COM

Bron Chapman

Bron is an enlivened new author who co-founded Elegchos, a non-profit created to address issues faced by youth with economic challenges. He has devoted several years to supporting youth in a variety of ways. He uses creativity to inspire youth to become adventure seekers, problem solvers, and to develop strong and open minds. He believes the world will always need innovative solutions and investing in children is a way to ensure these solutions will come to fruition. Bron lives in Texas with his wife Voncile; you can follow him on Instagram @boopscharactermissions.

John Chapman

Renaissance era, Cookie Tree, and Taj Mahal, what do they have in common? These are places John Chapman visited in his imagination through books as a child. Growing up in a small town in rural Mississippi, oftentimes without much to do, books provided a great avenue to dream and escape loneliness. John turned those desires into reality by visiting countries in 5 continents, mostly with his wife, Leslie. After spending many years in research and development, this is his first foray into co-authoring a children's book. John hopes to use this book and future ones to entertain, inspire, and encourage children's imaginations. He lives in Texas with his wife and three children. For more information on him and future books, you can follow him on Facebook @jchapman69.

Leslie Chapman

What drives Leslie Chapman to visit 4 continents and over 40 states in the U.S.? Her love for learning and travel. Besides family, these are her passions. As a former educator, teaching came with the job, but her experience extends beyond that, having taught wee ones up through seniors. It is in the fabric of who she is; and when she is playing with her three energetic toddlers, creative learning opportunities, often emerge. She lives in Texas with her husband John and children. To keep in touch with Leslie, follow her on Facebook @lchapman75.

Printed in the United States
By Bookmasters